W9-CBH-818

Harlem

a poem by

Walter Dean Myers

pictures by

Christopher Myers

Scholastic Inc.
New York Toronto London
Auckland Sydney

No part of this publication may be reproduced in whole or in part, or stored in a retrieval system, or transmitted in any form, or by any means, electronic, mechanical, photocopying, recording, or otherwise, without written permission of the publisher. For information regarding permission, write to Attention: Permissions Department, Scholastic Inc., 555 Broadway, New York, NY 10012.

ISBN 0-590-54341-5

Text copyright © 1997 by Walter Dean Myers.
Illustrations copyright © 1997 by Christopher Myers.
All rights reserved. Published by Scholastic Inc.

SCHOLASTIC and associated logos are trademarks and/or registered trademarks of Scholastic Inc.

12 11 10 9 8 7 6 5 4 3 2   8 9/9 0 1 2 3/0

Printed in the U.S.A.   08
First Scholastic paperback printing, September 1998

Book design by David Saylor. The art is a combination of ink, gouache, and collage.

The text is set in 14 point Franklin Gothic No. 2 Roman.

They took to the road in Waycross, Georgia

Skipped over the tracks in East St. Louis

Took the bus from Holly Springs

Hitched a ride from Gee's Bend

Took the long way through Memphis

The third deck down from Trinidad

A wrench of heart from Goree Island

A wrench of heart from Goree Island

To a place called Harlem

Harlem was a promise
Of a better life, of a place where a man didn't
Have to know his place
Simply because he was
Black

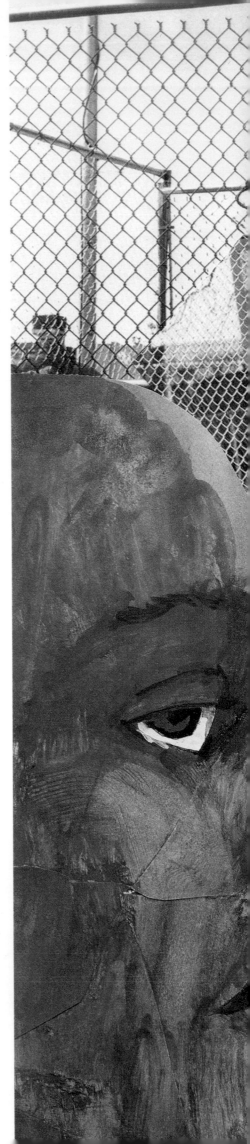

They brought a call, a song
First heard in the villages of
Ghana/Mali/Senegal
Calls and songs and shouts
Heavy hearted tambourine rhythms
Loosed in the hard city
Like a scream torn from the throat
Of an ancient clarinet

A new sound, raucous and sassy
Cascading over the asphalt village
Breaking against the black sky over
1-2-5 Street.
Announcing hallelujah
Riffing past resolution

Yellow/tan/brown/black/red
Green/gray/bright
Colors loud enough to be heard
Light on asphalt streets
Sun yellow shirts on burnt umber
Bodies
Demanding to be heard, seen
Sending out warriors

From streets that know to be
Mourning still as a lone radio tells us how Jack
Johnson/Joe Louis/Sugar Ray is doing with our
Hopes.

We hope, we pray
Our black skins
Reflecting the face of God
In storefront temples

Jive and Jehovah artists
Lay out the human canvas
The mood indigo

A chorus of summer herbs
Of mangoes and bar-b-que
Of perfumed sisters
Hip strutting past fried fish joints on
Lenox Avenue in steamy August

A carnival of children
People the daytime streets
Ring-a-levio warriors
Stickball heroes
Hide-and-seek knights and ladies
Waiting to sing their own sweet songs
Living out their own slam-dunk dreams
Listening
For the coming of the blues

A weary blues that Langston knew
And Countee sung
A river of blues where Du Bois waded
And Baldwin preached

There is lilt,
Tempo, cadence
A language of darkness
Darkness known
Darkness sharpened at Mintons
Darkness lightened at the Cotton Club
Sent flying from Abyssinian Baptist
To the Apollo.

The uptown A
Rattles past 110th Street
Unreal to real
Relaxing the soul

Shango and Jesus

Asante and Mende

One people, a hundred different

People

Huddled masses

And crowded dreams

Squares

Blocks, bricks

Fat/round woman in a rectangle

Sunday night gospel

      "Precious Lord...take my hand,

      Lead me on, let me stand..."

Caught by a full lipped, full hipped

Saint washing collard greens in a cracked

Porcelain sink

Backing up Lady Day on the radio

Brother so black and blue,
Patting a wide foot outside the too hot
Walk-up,
      "Boy, you ought to find the guy who told you
you could play some checkers 'cause he done lied
to you!"

Cracked reed/soprano sax laughter
Floats over a
Fleet of funeral cars.

In Harlem sparrows sit on fire escapes outside of
Rent parties to learn the tunes.
In Harlem the wind doesn't blow past Smalls, it
Stops to listen to the sounds.

Serious business, a poem/rhapsody tripping along
Striver's Row, not getting its metric feet soiled
On the well-swept walks
Hustling through the hard rain at two o'clock in
The morning to its next gig.

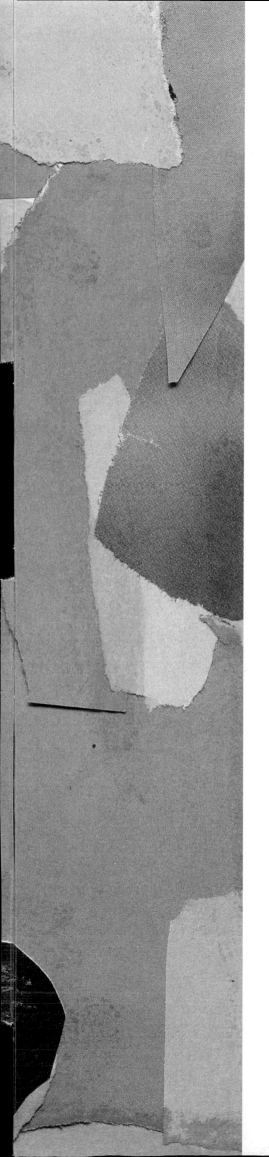

A huddle of horns and a tinkle of glass, a note
Handed down from Marcus to Malcolm to a brother
Too bad and too cool to give his name.

Sometimes despair makes
The stoops shudder
Sometimes there are endless depths of pain
Singing a capella on the street corners

And sometimes not.

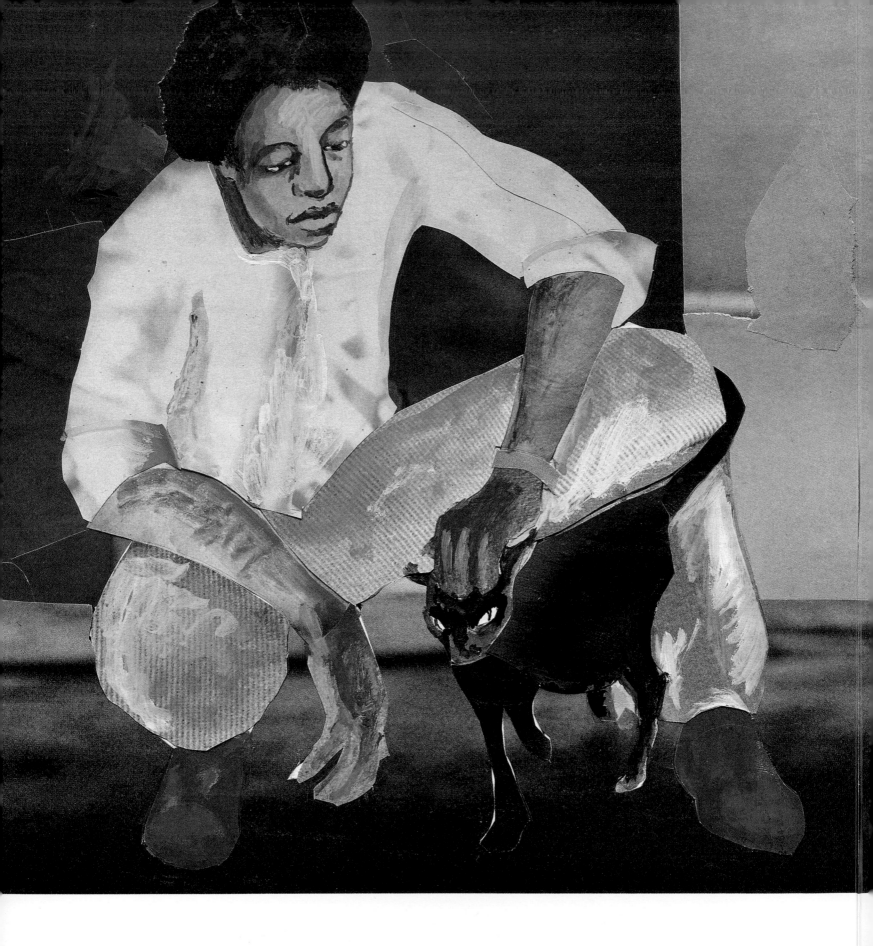

**Sometimes it is the artist looking into a mirror,
Painting a portrait of his own heart.**

Place, sound,
Celebration,
Memories of feelings, of place

A journey on the A train
That started on the banks of the Niger
And has not ended

Harlem.